Coastal Mississippi Alphabet

written by Rebecca M. Giles

illustrated by Liliya Todorova

To my parents Horace and Kay McMahon, my sister Melissa McMahon Butler and my husband Bryan Giles, who are my favorite Mississippians.

Special thanks to Karyn Tunks for her encouragement and guidance.

Can You Find Her?

Missy is an Atlantic Bottlenose Dolphin. These smart, social animals are called "bottlenose" because of their short, stubby snouts. They are the most common marine mammal in the Mississippi Sound and are often seen coming to the surface to breathe through their blowhole.

Missy is hidden in this book 12 times in different colors.

A is for aquarium with marine life on view welcoming visitors just like you.

The Mississippi Aquarium celebrates the state's unique marsh and gulf environments featuring salt and fresh water tanks along with exhibits of native plants and animals.

B

B is for beach with miles of white sand

LEAST TERN AREA

Nest in Peace

The longest man-made beach in the world stretches for 26 miles from Biloxi to Henderson Point. Constructed in 1951, the beach is a nesting paradise for the endangered Least Tern.

marking the place where water meets land.

Shallow water and gentle surf are ideal for swimming or riding the waves
on a kayak, paddleboard, sailboat, or water trike.

C is for cars cruising the coast.
Each one noticeably different from most.

Every October, antique, classic,
and hot rod vehicles drive the
beachside highway from
Bay St. Louis to Pascagoula.

D is for dolphins who jump and play
entertaining those met along the way.

The warm protected waters of the Mississippi Sound are home to one of
the world's largest stable populations of Atlantic Bottlenose Dolphins.

E is for estuary where river meets sea
creating a home for shrimp, turtles, and manatee.

The Grand Bay National Estuarine Research Reserve
is a protected area supporting a variety of fish and wildlife.

F is for Frenchmen who came to this shore.
Their stories are part of our history and lore.

In 1699, the first European settlement in Mississippi was established at Fort Maurepas, in present day Ocean Springs, by the French explorer Pierre Le Moyne d'Iberville and his brother Jean Baptiste de Bienville.

G is for George Ohr and his wild, wonderful pots.
No two are alike though he made quite a lot.

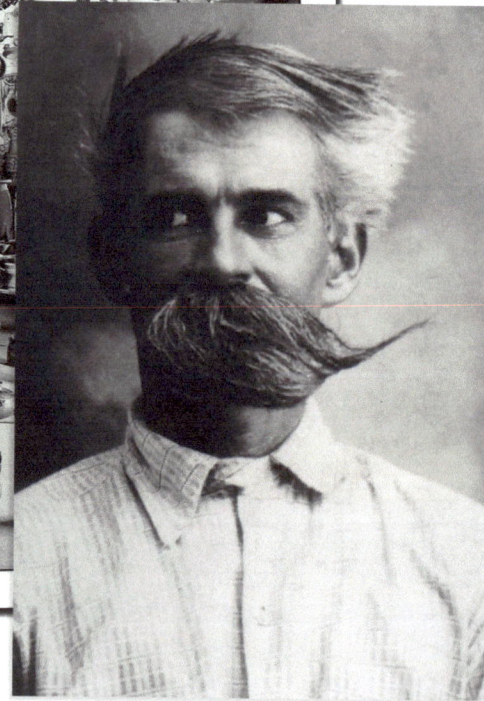

George E. Ohr, the "Mad Potter of Biloxi," is easily recognized by his 18-inch mustache and known for the vibrantly colored warped pitchers and twisted vases he created in the late 1800s.

H is for hurricanes that rage and blow leaving destruction wherever they go.

Mississippi Coast residents have endured two of the worst storms to ever hit North America, Camille (1969) and Katrina (2005).

I is for islands just off the coast.
They are best visited traveling by boat.

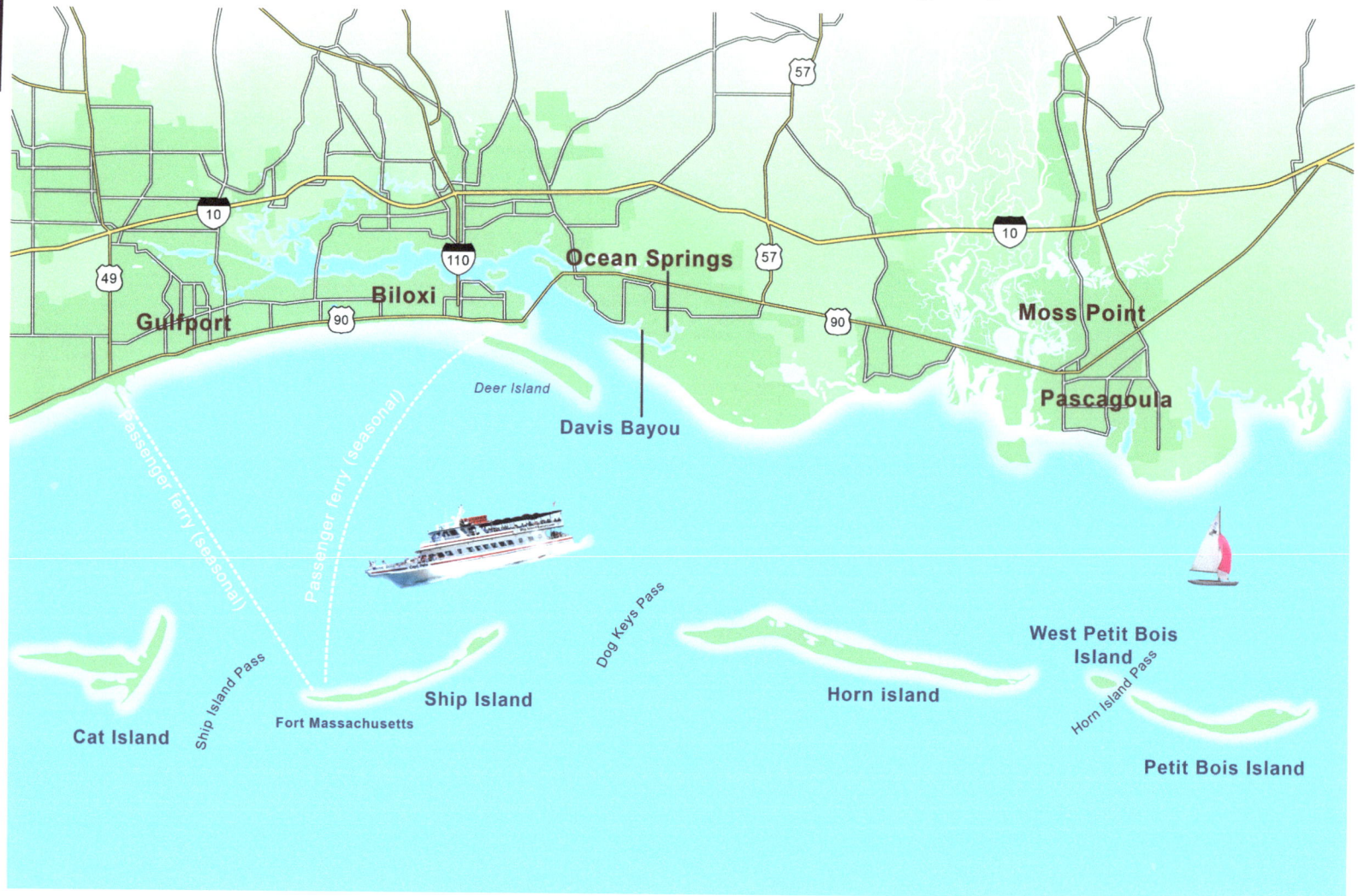

Deer Island

Davis Bayou

Gulfport

Biloxi

Ocean Springs

Moss Point

Pascagoula

Passenger ferry (seasonal)

Passenger ferry (seasonal)

Ship Island Pass

Cat Island

Fort Massachusetts

Ship Island

Dog Keys Pass

Horn island

West Petit Bois Island

Horn Island Pass

Petit Bois Island

The Mississippi Sound barrier islands, Cat, Ship, Horn, Petit Bois,
and West Petit Bois, are part of the Gulf Islands National Seashore.

J is for Jefferson Davis. As a young man, he did roam before making Beauvoir his last home.

"Beauvoir", Home of Jefferson Davis, Biloxi, Mississippi   135

Jefferson Davis served as a soldier, Congressman, Senator, U. S. Secretary of War, and as President of the Confederate States of America before living in Biloxi.

K

K is for Keesler that over the years has played host to service men and women stationed on the coast.

Keesler Air Force Base is home to the 81st Training Wing and 2nd Air Force as well as an Air Force Reserve unit commonly called the "Hurricane Hunters."

L is for lighthouse guiding the way
to keep ships and sailors from going astray.

Built in 1848, the cast-iron Biloxi Lighthouse was kept by the
Younghans family - husband, wife, and daughter - for 63 years.

M is for MGM Park. That's the stadium's name for watching a Shuckers baseball game.

MGM Park in Biloxi is home of a Minor League Baseball team whose name honors the Gulf Coast's oystering industry.

N

N is for nature found all around
where places for outdoor adventure abound.

The Coast's native environment includes beaches,
bays, rivers, creeks, swamps, marshes, islands, and piney woods.

O is for oysters grown where two shells meet creating a tasty saltwater treat.

Raw, fried, grilled, or stuffed oysters are a seafood staple in area restaurants.

P is for pelicans flying around, swooping and soaring then diving straight down.

Brown Pelicans, gulls, plovers, and sandpipers are among the shorebirds found along the coast.

Q is for queen reigning with her king over all the revelry Mardi Gras brings.

Mardi Gras is celebrated annually with lively parades, where riders throw spectators beads and other trinkets.

R is for root beer first made right here –
a traditional favorite that we hold dear.

Edward Charles Edmond Barq Sr. first bottled and sold the soda
that became Barq's Root Beer in 1898 through Biloxi Artesian Bottling Works.

S is for shrimper casting his net
never quite certain just what he'll get.

Brown, white, and pink shrimp are plentiful
close to the Mississippi Shore.

T is for tribes that we now know
lived here many long years ago.

"THE SINGING RIVER"

THE FAMOUS SINGING RIVER (PASCAGOULA) LOCATED ON U. S. 90 BETWEEN BILOXI, MISSIS-SIPPI AND MOBILE, ALABAMA IS KNOWN THROUGH THE WORLD FOR ITS VERY MYSTERIOUS MUSIC. THE SINGING SOUND, LIKE A SWARM OF BEES IN FLIGHT IS BEST HEARD IN LATE SUMMER AND AUTUMN MONTHS IN THE STILLNESS OF THE LATE EVENING. BARELY CAUGHT AT FIRST, THE MUSIC SEEMS TO GROW NEARER AND LOUDER UNTIL IT SOUNDS AS THOUGH IT COMES FROM DIRECTLY UNDER FOOT. AN OLD LEGEND CONNECTS THE SOUND WITH THE MYSTERIOUS EXTINCTION OF THE PASCAGOULA TRIBE OF INDIANS.   162

The Biloxi and Pascagoula were two of the Native American tribes living in Mississippi when the first Europeans arrived. Cities, bays, and rivers along the coast now have their names.

U is for underwater where many creatures are found swimming and crawling all around.

Fish, such as Amberjack, Cobia, Drum, Flounder, Mackerel, Mullet, Pompano, Red Fish, Scamp, Seatrout, and Tripletail, share the Mississippi coastal waters with crabs, jellyfish, sharks, and stingrays.

V is for veterans laid to rest
having given their country their very best.

Veterans from all branches of the United States Armed Forces are buried at the Biloxi National Cemetery. The Beauvoir Confederate Cemetery contains graves of Confederate veterans and their wives.

W

W is for Walter Anderson, an artist well-known for pictures of nature distinctly his own.

Walter Inglis Anderson made many trips to Horn Island by himself
to draw the plants and animals that appear in his block prints and watercolors.

X is for the crossing where you might wait as a train passes by loaded with freight.

Freight train activity along the coast is plentiful, creating the need for numerous railroad crossings.

Y is for yachting, a coastal sport with a proud history of sailed boats racing for victory.

Pass Christian, nicknamed the "Birthplace of Yachting in the South," hosted the region's first regatta in 1849. Today, there are seven members of the Mississippi Coast Yachting Association.

Z is for Zonta held each fall.
It's a day of festivities enjoyed by all.

Zonta of Pascagoula sponsors an annual arts and crafts festival
that brings vendors, food trucks, and live entertainment to the Downtown Plaza.

Glossary

Aquarium – Latin for "water place" and describes any size container where aquatic plants or animals are kept for display.

Estuary – Place where freshwater mixes with saltwater.

Freight – Cargo carried in a ship, plane, train or truck.

Hurricane – Tropical storm with winds over 74 miles per hour.

Least Tern – Small, endangered species of bird that flies low over water and catches tiny fish.

Lore – Traditions and knowledge held by a particular group of people.

Mardi Gras – French for "Fat Tuesday" and name for the holiday season that ends the day before Ash Wednesday.

Marsh - Soft, wet land covered by grasses or reeds.

Oystering – Harvesting oysters from the sandy bottom of shallow water either by hand or using a long-handled rake.

Petit Bois – French for "little wood" and pronounced like "petty bwa."

Regatta – A series of boat races.

Shucker – Nickname for a person who opens and removes oysters from their outer shells.

Veteran – Person who was once a soldier.

Yacht – Dutch (jacht) for "hunt" and originally, a navy name for a light, fast sailing vessel used to chase pirates. Today, it describes a boat used for pleasure or sport.

Zonta - Zonta International is a service organization with the mission of advancing the status of women world wide.

Acknowledgements

Photographs (Biloxi Artesian Bottle Works and men using oyster tongs) and vintage postcards (Beauvior, "The Singing River" and Keesler Air Field) Courtesy of the Local History and Genealogy Department of the Biloxi Public Library

Photographs of George Ohr Courtesy of the Ohr-O'Keefe Museum of Art

Photograph of Captain Pete Courtesy of Ship Island Excursions

Photograph of MGM Park taken by Katy Knauss Courtesy of Biloxi Shuckers Organization

Information for the T is for Tribe page courtesy of Amanda Ealy.

The Artist Rowing to Horn Island by Walter Inglis Anderson (1903-1965) c. 1960
Courtesy of the Walter Anderson Museum of Art and the Family of Walter Anderson

You can find Missy on the pages for the following letters: B, C, D, E, F, H, L, N, P, U, X and Z

www.ingramcontent.com/pod-product-compliance
Lightning Source LLC
Chambersburg PA
CBHW040404100426

42811CB00017B/1831